SPECIAL
by Kitt Chapman

Illustrations by Blueberry Illustrations

Copyright © 2017 by Kitt Chapman

All rights reserved.
No part of this book may be reproduced
or transmitted in any form or by any means
without written permission from the author.

ISBN-13: 978-1543233995
ISBN-10: 1543233996

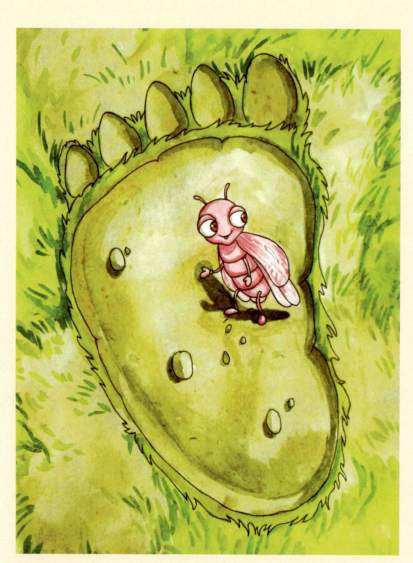

With heartfelt thanks to

Cosmos, for his unwavering support and encouragement along this journey,

Blueberry Illustrations, for the stellar art they created to help bring this story to life,

Humorist John Boston, for keeping me up all night at crunch time to edit, which wasn't funny at all,

My family, close friends, and 16 paws who are always there for me.

ALL kids are SPECIAL and some have SPECIAL NEEDS.

This book is dedicated to those dear and unique children.

Special was initially inspired after author Kitt Chapman was invited to Sunny View Public School in Toronto, Ontario, to share her music with a kindergarten class in 1994.

Her good friend, Ginny Walsh, at that time taught primary students, and had generously offered to be a 'test site' for Kitt's music.

The students in Ginny's class had various special needs. They touched Kitt in a way that can be best described as SPECIAL.

Ginny was a devoted teacher at Sunny View Public School for 19 years and is now enjoying her retirement as a spouse, mother and Nana, while raising a new puppy.

Thank you, Ginny, and all the other teachers, parents, and caregivers who are or have been involved with children who have special needs.

Was a ladybug
who had pink wings,

wondered why not
black-spotted red wings.

Realized
as time went by
her beautiful wings
helped her fly so high.

I'll rise up and touch the sky,
won't let a moment pass me by.
Look at me, I'm a specialty.
I am special and I love me.

Ladybug landed
on roly-poly bear.
Curiously
he had no hair.

Momma said
he was such a cute bear.

This is what he sang
as he looked in the mirror:

Look at me,
I'm a specialty.

I am special and I love me.

Ladybug and Bear
found a crooked old tree,

branches drooped,
he only had three.

Nothing ever bothered
to come so near.
Then came hope
and this song to cheer:

I'll rise up and touch the sky,
won't let a moment pass me by.
Look at me, I'm a specialty.
I am special and I love me.

Orange-breasted robin,
hiding in the tree,
listened as the others
sang like a symphony.

As hard as she tried,
her song came out wrong.

These friends loved it
and needed her along.

These friends loved it
and needed her along.

We'll rise up
and touch the sky,
won't let a moment
pass us by.

Look at us,
such a specialty,
we are special,
you and me.

We'll rise up
and touch the sky,
won't let a moment
pass us by.

ABOUT THE AUTHOR

Kitt Chapman, now retired and focusing on songwriting, was an Early Childhood Educator.

She has always loved music. At the age of six, she began her classical training on piano at the Royal Conservatory of Music. At summer camp, she taught herself the guitar around the campfire. She sang in the church choir, played the cello and violin in high school, and dibbled a dabbled in miscellaneous other instruments, including the flute and the harp.

After raising her three wonderful children, she had time to pursue songwriting.

Asked what inspired her to write songs, she commented, "I thrive on creating music and lyrics, ultimately to enhance storytelling. Preschoolers have such vivid imaginations, and to be able to tap into that space brings me much happiness. If I can engage and develop their musicality, even briefly, I feel I've succeeded in my quest."

Parents and teachers alike are moved and delighted by the lyrics and melodies of Kitt's children's songs. There is a balance of education and fun.

Another port for this prolific songwriter is adult focused. Ranging from instrumental to lyrical compositions, her themes imbue a respect for humanity and nature.

Kitt's latest project is creating, producing and hosting a children's radio show, for kids aged ten and under, called KittsKids.RadioRomp.

To follow Kitt and her music, please visit webpage:
www.kittchapman.me

SPECIAL is the first 'sing-along' book Kitt has published. We are hopeful there will be many more to come!

Made in the USA
Middletown, DE
17 March 2017